# THE TWELVE STEPS

An Interpretation of

# THE TWELVE STEPS

of the

# ALCOHOLICS ANONYMOUS PROGRAM

COLL-WEBB CO., PUBLISHERS

P. O. Box 564

Minneapolis, Minnesota                    MCMXLVI

*The Little Red Book: The Original 1946 Edition*

Reprinted by:
The Full Length History Press
flh-press.blogspot.com
full.length.history.press@gmail.com

No copyright claimed by The Full Length History Press

ISBN: 978-1491209967
1491209968

The Full Length History Press is not affiliated with Alcoholics Anonymous World Services, Inc., the General Service Office of Alcoholics Anonymous, the Hazelden Foundation, or Hazelden Publishing. The publication of this book has not been authorized or endorsed by, and does not imply affiliation with Alcoholics Anonymous World Services, Inc., the General Service Office of Alcoholics Anonymous, the Hazelden Foundation, or Hazelden Publishing.

*Bibliographical Note:*
In order to facilitate study by the broadest possible audience, pagination has been altered to correspond to the fourth edition of *Alcoholics Anonymous*. No other changes have been made to the original text.

**This book is sold at printing cost, in an effort to carry the message to alcoholics. The Full Length History Press makes no money from its sale.**

# CONTENTS

## Author's Note

*This book was originally prepared as a series of notes for Twelve-step Discussion meetings for new A. A. members. It proved to be very effective and helpful. Many groups adopted it, using mimeographed copies. The demand for this interpretation in book form from both individuals and groups made printing advisable.*

Published by Coll-Webb Company
Minneapolis, Minnesota

# DEDICATION

This interpretation is sincerely dedicated to

## BILL & DR. BOB

in appreciation of their tireless efforts and inspiration in making possible a WAY OF LIFE by which alcoholics everywhere can recover from alcoholism.

The endless thousands who have recovered from this disease and those who are yet to be helped will ever be indebted to the founders of ALCOHOLICS ANONYMOUS for the unselfish service they have rendered all alcoholics.

We believe our founders were inspired by a POWER GREATER THAN THEMSELVES as they pioneered the Alcoholics Anonymous movement, edited the book, "Alcoholics Anonymous" and exemplified the spiritual philosophy of this recovery program.

# INTRODUCTION

This introduction to the Twelve Steps of the Alcoholics Anonymous program is humbly offered to all alcoholic men and women whose "lives have become unmanageable" because of their powerlessness over alcohol.

The purpose of the interpretation that follows is to help the newcomer in his study and application of the Twelve Steps of A. A. This interpretation is founded upon fundamental information taken from our book, "Alcoholics Anonymous."

All supplementary matter is based on practical experience from the lives of fellow alcoholics who have found peace of mind and contented sobriety by a planned way of spiritual life set forth in the book, "Alcoholics Anonymous."

The newcomer, too often, fails to realize the extent to which he is physically, mentally and spiritually ill, so through ignorance dwarfs parts of our program to suit his own distorted viewpoint.

It is obvious that much good can be accomplished by imparting to the new member the fund of knowledge which successful older members have gained by experience. The intent of this introduction and the object of this interpretation is toward that end.

The A. A. program by which we effect our recovery is extremely simple. It would need little interpretation in itself, except for the fact that it corrects a highly complicated disease which has lowered our physical resistance, distorted our thinking, and rendered us spiritually ill.

Few uncontrolled drinkers realize the danger of their position or the great extent to which the disease alcoholism can damage and deteriorate their minds and bodies. Few realize the full significance and effectiveness of our simple program without the help and cooperation of understanding members who have arrested their alcoholism.

A. A. has no connection with organized religion, medicine or psychology. It has drawn upon certain therapeutic virtues from them all, however, and has moulded them into a "Design for Living" that has returned us to sobriety and restored us to a place of service and respect in society.

The A.A. program is designed for uncontrolled drinkers who sincerely desire permanent sobriety and are willing to go to any lengths to get it. Men or women interested in temporary sobriety or in controlling their drinking are not ready for this program.

The ability to be honest is a most necessary requirement following the desire of the new member for rehabilitation. Willingness to get well, and belief in a POWER GREATER THAN OURSELVES to promote recovery, are essentials necessary to success.

Spiritual concepts must be embraced, but again we say they do not involve organized religion and although you must believe in this POWER yet it is your privilege to interpret it in accordance with your own understanding.

The alcoholics who have recovered through the Alcoholics Anonymous movement nationally disprove the age-old contention that all alcoholics are untrustworthy, and that they are destined to remain hopeless, drunken sots. Thousands upon thousands have disproved this, and hundreds of new alcoholics are daily proving that by living the A.A. philosophy, alcoholism can be arrested.

Permanent sobriety is the aim of the A.A. philosophy, but that in itself is not enough, for with it we must become contented, happy, responsible people.

The Twelve Steps of the A.A. program have provided us with a sound, proved means for recovery; we have yet to meet an alcoholic who, honestly desirous of arresting his alcoholism, and following the Twelve Steps as interpreted, did not recover.

It is true certain drinkers have not succeeded. A few of the reasons for their failures are listed.

1. Some sought our help to appease their wives, employers, judge, or to avoid impending evils that prolonged drinking develops. Theirs was a temporary problem. We have nothing to offer such people until they are definitely qualified as alcoholics and desire to stop drinking.

2. Those who have suffered brain injury from alcohol. (Symptomatic drinkers.)

3. Some failed because they were dope addicts— they drank, yes—but alcohol was not their basic problem.

4. Some were forced into the movement; they lacked sincerity, so did not last.

5. Some were heavy drinkers, but not alcoholics. They were not mentally or physically *one* of the *seven in every one thousand* adults who were abnormal reactors to alcohol.

6. The occasional atheist who is unwilling to accept the spiritual concept which underlies the A.A. program. (See Appendix 2 of A.A. book.)

7. The alcoholic who is constitutionally dishonest has no chance. He cannot be honest with himself.

8. Those who have not been harmed sufficiently by alcohol often fail because drinking is not a matter of life and death with them. This group

generally involves the men and women with relatively short alcoholic histories.

9. Those who accept only a part of the Twelve-Step Program, who will not try to live it in its entirety. Those who wish to put a distorted, selfish interpretation on all of the steps for purposes of their own convenience.

The prospective member who falls under any of the groups listed, *with the exception* of group 8, has little chance of recovery.

Prospective members shown under group 8 need not be unduly alarmed if they are alcoholic and sincerely desire to recover. They can be as successful as any other member. They simply happen to be in a group that has had more difficulty than those in the more advanced ages. Their cue is—be on the alert.

Some people reason along the line that although they are not alcoholic, that alcoholism could be avoided by belonging to an A.A. group. This is questionable, for it is not until the alcoholic has punished himself and family severely that he gives serious thought to the arresting of his alcoholism. Even then he must prove to himself that he "can't take it." It takes consistent pounding of our heads against the rough wall of alcoholism before we are convinced.

For those who are willing to accept this program, and can qualify as alcoholics, we advise you to make a close study of our book, "Alcoholics Anonymous." Read it repeatedly.

This book has all your answers; it was written by alcoholics for alcoholics and based on the trials and experiences of the first 100 Alcoholics Anonymous members. They worked out a recovery program that has proved sound and effective.

By using it as your text book, regularly attending A.A. meetings, and referring to the interpretations of the Twelve Steps, as you progress, you will lay a strong foundation upon which you can rehabilitate your life.

We are not disturbed by the realization that strict adherence to this program demands perfection. We know perfection is impossible. We merely strive toward perfecting ourselves in a way of life that is necessary to bring permanent sobriety, happiness and well-being to uncontrolled drinkers.

# The Twelve Steps

STEP ONE—*Admitted that we were powerless over alcohol and that our lives had become unmanageable.*

STEP TWO—*Came to believe that a Power Greater than Ourselves could restore us to sanity.*

STEP THREE—*Made a decision to turn our will and our lives over the care of God as we understand Him.*

STEP FOUR—*Made a searching and fearless moral inventory of ourselves.*

STEP FIVE—*Admitted to God, to ourselves and to another human being the exact nature of our wrongs.*

STEP SIX—*We were entirely ready to have God remove all these defects of character.*

STEP SEVEN—*Humbly ask Him to remove our shortcomings.*

STEP EIGHT—*Made a list of all the people we had harmed and become willing to make amends to them all.*

STEP NINE—*Made direct amends to such people whereever possible, except when to do so would injure them or others.*

STEP TEN—*Continued to take personal inventory and when we were wrong promptly admitted it.*

STEP ELEVEN—*Sought through prayer and meditation to improve our conscious contact with God as we understood Him, praying only for knowledge of His will for us and the power to carry that out.*

STEP TWELVE—*Having had a spiritual experience as the result of these steps, we tried to carry this message to alcoholics, and to practice these principles in all our affairs.*

**STEP ONE**—*Admitted that we were powerless over alcohol and that our lives had become unmanageable*

————

Men and women who are allergic to alcohol and who compulsively persist in its use as a beverage eventually become ill from a unique disease. This disease is known to medicine as alcoholism; it is unique in that it adversely affects one physically, mentally and spiritually.

Step One briefly portrays the pathetic enigma of an uncontrolled drinker who has acquired this illness over which he is entirely powerless.

Drinkers of this type consider alcohol a physical requirement; they gradually increase its consumption at the expense of proper intake of nutritious foods. This practice induces physical and nervous disorders decidedly unfavorable to their comfort and health.

The study of Step One will be confined to the physical illness induced by alcoholism.

Few alcoholics have given their drinking problem much intelligent study. They reluctantly agree they must quit but keep right on drinking.

Severe "hangovers" make them realize that physical illness plays a part in their discomfort but a little "hair off the dog that bit them" is resorted to and they either continue on into a new binge or finally taper off under the suffering of much physical and mental anguish.

The alcoholic lives in a self-imposed slavery, as alcohol provides the only means he knows by which life is made bearable, or by which he can appease his jittery nerves. Existence under such circumstances soon make his life unmanageable.

Correction of this condition is a serious problem of immediate concern. The seeming futility of making a satisfactory adjustment to the environment of normal, sober living can be accomplished, however, if we are sincere in our desire to permanently divorce our lives from alcohol.

The founders of Alcoholics Anonymous identified their powerlessness over alcohol as "the inability to leave it alone no matter how great the necessity or wish." They outlined a remedy in the form of a Twelve-Step Program. This program amounts to a "WAY OF LIFE." It restores the alcoholic to health and sobriety, bringing to him a heretofore unknown peace of mind and happiness.

By trial and error the founders worked out the details of a simple but sure philosophy for recovery from alcoholism. Recovery is possible but a cure cannot be effected. The man or woman who has become an alcoholic can never become a controlled drinker. To drink again would continue a progressive illness. Continued use of alcohol brings on increased susceptibility to the drug rather than physical or mental resistance.

The first things of importance to consider in our recovery from the narcotic influence of alcohol are:

1. We must have a sincere desire to stop drinking.
2. We must admit and believe in our innermost hearts that we are powerless over this drug.
3. We must classify alcohol as a slow but deadly poison.
4. We must consider ourselves as patients in A.A. for treatment.
5. We must look upon alcoholism as a disease of the body, mind and spirit.
6. We must make it our business to understand how alcohol affects the alcoholic.
7. We must realize we are alcoholics.
8. We must learn and practice the Twelve Steps of the A.A. program.
9. We must believe that we can arrest our alcoholism, but that we can never drink again.
10. We must take on a layman's knowledge of alcoholism insofar as it affects our health and mentality.
11. We must use this knowledge and understanding of our disease not only to gain sobriety

> but also to guard against future danger of a return to drinking.
>
> 12. We must do this partially by keeping in our minds a mental picture of the unmanageable life alcohol demands from us and our powerlessness over it.

The layman's view and understanding of alcoholism is a simple one based on a few facts and backed up with his own experiences plus the knowledge gained from contact with other alcoholics. The following discussion of alcoholism briefly covers the facts necessary to a beginner who will naturally increase his understanding as he makes the Alcoholics Anonymous program his "WAY OF LIFE."

Nature has provided each normal man and woman with a physical body designed to withstand the rigors of a strenuous daily life.

A healthy person can endure great hardships under most unfavorable circumstances so long as he receives oxygen, water, balanced nutrition, proper rest and relaxation. The human tenacity to retain that "spark of life" is persistent as long as we do not withhold these requisites.

When any one of them are permanently withheld we set up conditions that nature cannot long endure. Sooner or later deficiencies occur in our bodies, nervous tension and neurotic conditions are established; our nervous systems upset mental balance and we eventually die from lack of rest and nourishment.

Alcoholism stimulates such a condition and further complicates it by a systematic daily intake of toxic poison—alcohol.

This takes place first in the blood stream; later in the brain, as we progressively deplete our blood and body cells of sufficient nutrition, sugar, vitamins and minerals by substituting in their places the poison alcohol.

This poison irritates the complex organism of the brain and finally breaks down nature's defensive barriers of protection. Physical deterioration is sometimes quite rapid but, in most alcoholics, alcoholism is acquired over a period of years, so it is only in the later stages of the disease that acute physical breakdown is apparent.

For this reason the alcoholic remains ignorant of his real trouble. He is incapable of visualizing his dangerous physical or mental condition because his mental faculties have been gradually inhibited as the transformation from alcohol as a social stimulant to a physical need increases.

Others notice the change but the alcoholic remains ignorant of his true condition and vainly tries to interpret life from his alcoholic point of view rather than from the reality and conventions of a normal world.

Freedom from alcoholism, which is responsible for our unmanageable lives, can only be accomplished when we remove the cause of our illness and return to a permanent, regular, balanced diet that completely eliminates alcohol. There is no short cut; no substitution; no other way out for the alcoholic.

Controlled drinkers have no trouble conforming to this procedure but the uncontrolled drinker who has lowered his physical resistance and shattered his nervous system should have medical help and care before he starts to effect his rehabilitation.

Many members who ignore the importance of their physical well-being as an asset to recovery will fail to arrest their alcoholism. Some may recover but they slow up the process if they do not feel well physically.

We believe that all alcoholics should be hospitalized upon their request for help from Alcoholics Anonymous. This is not possible in all cases so the members who cannot receive hospital care are cautioned to consult a competent doctor who is skilled in the diagnosis of alcoholism.

The importance of this advice cannot be over-emphasized. The alcoholic is a sick man. He does not realize it and wishes to minimize his physical condition. This should not be allowed by the older members; they should point out the need of a complete physical check-up and see that the new member gets it.

Those who neglect the simple precaution of receiving ethical medical care are not honest in their desire to effect a speedy recovery from alcoholism.

The alcoholic, whose life has become unmanageable from uncontrolled drinking, is taking a serious step when he identifies himself with our program and attempts to make it his "WAY OF LIFE." His future security depends on the successful attainment of A.A. as a "WAY OF LIFE." He cannot allow impaired physical well-being to detract from his chances of recovery, therefore he must safeguard his health, as poor health may return him to drinking.

The new member will do well to investigate the various phases of alcoholism that apply to his case; he should admit that he is an alcoholic and discuss his problems with older members who are always willing to offer advice and render help.

Learn to see in alcoholism a diseased condition of the nervous system due to the excessive use of alcohol. Reflect upon your powerlessness over this disease. Learn a number of the tests in the medical and psychological field that identify alcoholics. Admit that you "can't take it." Consider your inability to "take it or leave it alone;" remember that your inability to leave it alone, in the face of impending disaster if you take it, definitely marks you as an alcoholic. The necessity of a drink "the morning after" is common to most alcoholics. There are many other identifications of the alcoholic—make it your business to learn some of them.

The founders of Alcoholics Anonymous understood that the member would have to realize his physical illness and receive medical help before he could fully employ his mental faculties on the spiritual requirements necessary to our program. Physical health is a necessity but only an asset to the real help we receive in recovery from our alcoholic illness.

Step Two gives us an indication of the sort of help our founders resorted to in returning themselves to sanity which is the next step of the A.A. program.

STEP TWO–*Came to believe that a Power Greater than Ourselves could restore us to sanity*

———

The purpose of this step is to disclose the nature of the mental illness which we have suffered from alcoholism and to admit the belief we can overcome it by help from a POWER GREATER THAN OURSELVES.

The mental disability of the alcoholic is self-imposed; it is grounded in self-centeredness which is nurtured by the narcotic alcohol, over which we are powerless. Exhaustive research from the cases of thousands of alcoholics who have arrested their illness, point conclusively to the fact that will power is not a factor in treatment except when the will of the individual is surrendered to a POWER GREATER THAN HIS OWN.

Those of us who have had an honest desire to recover from the mental sickness that alcoholism has imposed upon us have successfully used t h i s POWER. We refer to it as the POWER OF GOD and recommend it to all alcoholics as a source of healing. It renews the mind as it straightens out our thinking.

What you call this POWER is a matter of your own choice; call it what you will; its recovery value lies in the fact you believe IT exists; that you approach IT with a faith and that you sincerely depend upon IT to restore you to mental fitness.

Harmony with God is the only hope of the alcoholic; it is possible by making A.A. your way of life. The acceptance and practice of the Twelve Steps of the A.A. program will give you a conscious contact with this Power Greater than Yourself; it will restore you to sane thinking.

The inability of the uncontrolled drinker to be self critical often causes him to waste time in useless discussion of the use of the word sanity in Step Two. He is willing to concede his physical and spiritual illness but objects to any question of his mental soundness. We offer the following explanation for members with such opinions.

The beginner will avoid confusion in his interpretation of this step if he approaches it with a sincere desire for the accepted A.A. meaning. Remind yourself that you are making the A.A. recovery program your way of life because it is essential to your recovery from alcoholism. On it depends the well-being of your mind and body; your happiness and the security of your home—your very life. It might very well be suicide to disagree with any part of it, so resolve to accept the Twelve Steps in their entirety.

Some members have eventually arrived at the true meaning of Step Two by temporarily rephrasing it to read, "Came to believe that a POWER GREATER THAN OURSELVES could restore us to sane behavior."

The truth of the matter is that the great majority of our members have only acted on the level of insanity during periods of intoxication. This is common practice to all drinkers who get "tight," but to the alcoholic who shortens the intervals between his periods of intoxication and finally merges them into one long "drunk," it becomes a serious matter. Insane behavior because of an evening's drinking is generally excused, but when carried on for weeks and months that lengthen into years, it becomes a fixed pattern that is sponsored by the brain.

We cannot overlook the harmful effect of the prolonged use of alcohol on the brain or that it does produce an unhealthy mental condition which results in a complacent disregard of sane thought or normal behavior. The alcoholic cannot control his impulses; he lacks mental coordination; continued use of the drug damages the brain and in some cases brings on insanity.

Various degrees of brain injury exists in all alcoholics in proportion to their physical resistance to alcohol poisoning and to the length of time involved in abnormal drinking.

The alcoholic who wishes to cling to the illusion that he exercised sanity in his drinking is invited to prove his case against the accepted definition of insanity.

"A simple definition for insanity is a disorder of conduct that occurs when the body impulses no longer find in the brain a coordinating center for the conditioning of conduct. When this condition arises man's behavior is unpredictable and he becomes legally insane."

The behavior of the uncontrolled drinker who has become alcoholic is likewise unpredictable and his friends and relatives take on a long face as alcoholism perverts his power of reason; dulls his talent; limits his instinct of self preservation; makes him irresponsible; and adversely affects his behavior.

How is the alcoholic to account for that insane impulse which prompts him to reach for the FIRST DRINK that starts him off on another "binge?"

Is it a sane act? Is he obsessed? Is it the result of an urge which is sponsored by irrational thinking? Does it involve thinking?

Does sanity in an alcoholic implicate his power to accept or reject that FIRST DRINK?

We think it does as we do not believe that he can help himself. We believe and know from experience that a POWER GREATER THAN HIMSELF can remove his obsession; straighten out his thinking; and restore him to sane thought and behavior.

Those who disapprove the use of the word sanity in Step Two are usually alcoholics who have been fortunate enough to escape the more serious aspects of alcoholism. They reason that they were perfectly normal between drinking bouts.

The alcoholic who did himself no serious damage during his drinking career should find solace in that fact. He should take a broad view of the insanity of alcoholism, however, as most of us were surely deranged over varying periods of time.

He must also remember that in the progressive development of alcoholism the power of reasoning is slowly demoralized. This encourages deception as to our real mental health and fitness; it breeds a superior feeling of false security.

Evidence to support this fact is found in the following danger symptoms commonly seen in all alcoholics:

1.  Acceptance of that FIRST DRINK as we minimize the knowledge of the physical and mental suffering of the past by saying, "THIS TIME IT WILL BE DIFFERENT."

2. The continued use of alcohol to escape the realities of life and dependence upon it for energy or courage to accomplish given work.

3. The necessity of the drink "the morning after."

4. Our inability to be self-critical of the sanity of our behavior over prolonged years of drinking–our refusal to consider the harm we have done to ourselves and others.

5. Childish faith we placed in excuses for our drinking and the alibis we thought we were getting away with.

6. The reckless abandon we displayed in drunken driving–the argument that we drive better drunk than sober and our resentment toward those who differed from this opinion.

7. The acute physical condition we reach and the continued suffering we endure from uncontrolled drinking.

8. The financial risks taken–the shame, sorrow and often poverty that we inflict upon our families.

9. The asinine resentments that clogged our minds–our decided loss of responsibility–our retreats to childish levels of hilarity–the erroneous assumption that we can "take it or leave it alone"–our unnecessary squandering of money.

These are a few of the infinite number of danger symptoms that indict alcohol as poison to alcoholic men and women, and prove that their power of reason is affected, as well as their behavior, when even small doses of this drug are consumed.

There is no point in deceiving ourselves regarding the fate of the alcoholic, the uncontrolled drinker, if he continues to use alcohol. He has just two escapes from drinking, one is insanity; the other is alcoholic death. The purpose of the A.A. program as a "Way of Life" is to avoid both by arresting the disease alcoholism.

As alcoholics we cannot undo our past behavior; we can, however, use the knowledge of our escape from insanity and alcoholic death as an incentive to contact God for help in keeping us from future drinking.

It is now our privilege to draw on the help of a POWER GREATER THAN OURSELVES to bring us to our senses. The alcoholic record of our past life is not the basis upon which our future will be judged. We have a new page before us; we are invited to "write our own ticket." Sobriety, sanity, security and peace of mind are within our reach.

The future, with the A.A. program as "OUR WAY OF LIFE," will bring us sane, useful, happy lives. We have learned our lesson; namely, that for us alcohol is poison that brings mental illness and insane behavior.

Surely, with this knowledge, we can never lay claim to sanity if we again take THAT FIRST DRINK.

STEP THREE–*Made a decision to turn our will and our lives over to the care of God as we understand Him*

––––––––

The objective of the study of Steps One, Two and Three is to identify in alcoholism a three-fold disease that has made inroads upon our physical health, our mental capacity and our spiritual happiness and well-being.

A complete knowledge of the injury we have suffered at the hands of "John Barleycorn" is indispensable to our recovery from alcoholism.

The purpose of Step Three is to recognize and treat a malady none of us formerly looked upon as a disease; this malady is spiritual illness. A.A., as a "Way of Life," is basically a spiritual program that arrests alcoholism as we develop within ourselves a true sense of responsibility to God and to those we have harmed by our uncontrolled drinking.

Knowledge and treatment of our physical and mental sickness are necessary but we never attain full recovery until we conquer our spiritual sickness.

As uncontrolled drinkers we have lived our lives willfully and selfishly bringing unhappiness, trouble and disgrace upon ourselves. Our powerlessness over alcohol outweighed the regard we held for our own security or the good intentions toward our loved ones.

The remorse that drinking brought filled us with kindly intent toward deserving friends and relatives, but never allowed us to make permanent restitution. Resolutions and good intentions bolstered great faith within us during periods of sobriety, but being spiritually ill, we were unable to carry out our plans. Our "dog house" existence was occasionally relieved by sane and thoughtful acts during sober moments only to be resumed upon the next drunk, until we lost faith in ourselves. We were strong willed in all matters except in our ability to control our drinking; our drinking behavior; or our treatment of others.

It is not until we are fully aware of these facts that we become "fed up" with our inability to assume or execute normal responsibilities. It is only when we realize and admit the fact that "Our troubles were self imposed and that we were extreme examples of self will run riot" that we are ready to look outside ourselves for help.

Alcoholics who have accepted and practiced Step Three know the value of turning their will and their lives over to the care of God as they understand Him. Faith in the power of God, as they under-

stand Him, has brought them happiness and sobriety as it promoted recovery from the spiritual illness of alcoholism.

Some of us hesitated to face the requirements of
this step for fear of public opinion or because
it seemed hypocritical to turn to God for help after
ignoring Him for years.

It is well to realize that we belong to an anonymous society; that the public has no way of knowing
what we are doing *except that we no longer drink*.
The fact is that although they did not accept us
while we drank, they will honor and receive us
when we stop.

We failed to stop of our own volition; we tried
devious way of controlling our drinking and to
regulate our lives; we have done everything within
our power and knowledge to escape the effects of
alcoholism.

The sensible thing to do now, if we are serious
about gaining permanent sobriety, is to surrender
our false pride, as thousands of other alcoholics
have done, and effect our recovery from alcoholism
under the care of GOD as we understand Him. The
fact these thousands of alcoholics have recovered
and that new hundreds are daily doing it by help
from a POWER GREATER THAN OURSELVES

should leave no doubt about our chances of recovery.

Those of us who claim it hypocritical to now turn to God and ask for help because of alcoholic problems are still avoiding responsibility. We know what should be done about the matter but are not being honest with ourselves when we refuse to accept His help. Our reasoning is still along the line of escape from reality; we are still dealing in the alibi of the alcoholic.

The sort of reasoning will continue our insane behavior and spiritual illness as it leads back to our former practices. We must accept the need and authenticity of each step in the Alcoholics Anonymous program if we are to make it a "WAY OF LIFE."

There is no provision in any of the Twelve Steps that justifies the questioning of God's willingness to extend help for your recovery, providing you are sincere in your determination to get well.

Self-surrender of fear, pride, resentment, egotism, willfulness and all the undesirable traits that make up the personality of the alcoholic must be submitted to the care of God for supervision and constructive reconditioning.

Forgetting the seemingly overwhelming importance of our alcoholic problems, we must learn to rely on His power. Reliance on self-will becomes less difficult to renounce when we consider the part it has played in "messing up our lives."

Think for a minute of the futility of self-centered alcoholic living; recall the emptiness and suffering of alcoholic-inspired self-exaltation; remember the defeat and despair it brought us, the ill health, the irrational thinking and behavior of the alcoholic.

We must agree that any will, other than our own, could have regulated our affairs to better advantage. Surely we have been kidding ourselves long enough. It is time to take on an understanding of God's will and make ourselves a channel for its expression.

We have before us the examples of A.A. members who are doing their best to learn the meaning of God's will and to constantly draw on HIS power for help. It is interesting to note that these members have exchanged their old alcoholic personalities for the sober, happy personality of the sincere A.A. member.

Honesty, humility and willingness to establish an alert consciousness of this POWER GREATER THAN OURSELVES is the first requirement in trying to understand God.

Success in improving our conscious contact with God results from faith in HIS power; from meditation; from prayer; from observation of members whom you feel have made a contact with HIM; from discussion of Step Three with such members.

We get nowhere trying to force a contact or understanding. It must come naturally as we surrender our problems to HIM. We gain an understanding of this matter as we unselfishly go about the business of understanding another fellow's problem and trying to help him. God often shows us the answer to our own problem through solution of the other fellows difficulties. The faith we practice with relaxed patience as we work out the Twelve Steps of the A. A. program assures us an understanding of this POWER GREATER THAN OURSELVES.

The new members should not confuse any part of the Alcoholics Anonymous philosophy with his church or organized religion. The fact he is willing to turn his will and life over to the care of God as he understands Him is a spiritual concept of our program necessary for the rehabilitation of the alcoholic.

Religious views are things to be dealt with outside of A.A. Your conception of GOD AS YOU UNDERSTAND HIM; the fact that you believe in a POWER GREATER THAN YOURSELF to restore you to spiritual health is all that our program requires.

"As soon as a man says he does believe or is willing to believe, we emphatically assure him that he is on his way.

"It has been repeatedly proved among us that upon this simple cornerstone a wonderful effective spiritual structure can be built."

Belief and faith in God are necessary to the alcoholic; in them he finds the solution of a happy, sober life. They bring him peace of mind; an active, useful life; strength and understanding to combat his daily problems; the power to resist alcohol; the ability to develop mental and spiritual health; the opportunity to amend his past errors.

Few newcomers need any introduction to the idea of a Divine Being. Most of us were taught this in our youth. We have all seen evidence of a POWER GREATER THAN OURSELVES in our well-regulated world of fixed seasons, dominated by day and night; by heat and moisture; peopled by the reproduction of human life and made livable by the love and tolerance of human beings.

Most of us have studied the perfection of the universe; the animation of living things; the action of the human mind; the power of love. These things all seem to denote a dynamic life force, back of, in and through everything about us. This force appears to direct all things harmoniously but irresistibly toward a natural, definite, useful conclusion.

It is not hard to recognize in this Life Force a POWER GREATER THAN OURSELVES. In it we feel creative energy and sense, intelligence and power that makes man most insignificant by comparison.

He remains insignificant so long as he ignores the POWER, but becomes a source of constructive energy when he identifies himself with it and makes himself an agent for its fulfillment.

We identify ourselves with this Life Force; this POWER GREATER THAN OURSELVES when we:

1. Assume an attitude of surrender of self-centered interests.
2. Assume a humble attitude of faith backed by sincere desire for sobriety.
3. Assume the willingness to pray unselfishly.
4. Assume and believe that we are spiritually ill.
5. Assume the responsibility of overcoming our illness.
6. Make a decision to place our will and life in God's care for treatment.
7. Pray without resentment in our hearts.
8. Consider the positive things that lead away from past moral defects.

9. Sense the necessity of cleanliness of heart.
10. Become forgiving of others.
11. Recognize the spiritual potentialities within us.
12. Try to understand God with a view toward developing these potentialities.

The important thing is our willingness to TRY. Every man and woman has spiritual possibilities. We must learn to bring them out, to form convictions and let them grow.

When it is possible we should take our wives or close relatives into our confidence as we attempt to carry out the provision of this step. We have found that there is great strength and help to the member who has the confidence and cooperation of those close to him. If they are not cooperative he must work it out alone.

We should avoid the common mistake of confusing our minds with anxious thoughts regarding the time and manner God will manifest Himself to us. Our understanding will come gradually as we earn and develop it.

It is uncommon for a member to have a drastic spiritual upheaval. Spiritual awakening or experience comes slowly and often in strange ways. It does come, however, but so naturally that we many times fail to recognize it.

Our job is to be ready and willing for these experiences, to take an incentive from the example of fellow members who are living the A.A. program; to be open-minded in our approach to understand God; to realize that it is not made up of one big accomplishment but is gained bit by bit, and that our inspiration will be influenced by our attitude and action. The active member who takes the program seriously by applying it to his home life; in his business; in the treatment of new members; by admitting wrongs and by making amends is most likely to suddenly realize the presence of God in his life.

Quiet periods of relaxation and prayer are most necessary to the achievement of this step. The alcoholic should also keep in mind the value of relaxation aside from prayer. He should not overlook the fact that all alcoholics are of restless disposition; that restlessness and tension are a part of their trouble; that we once appeased this condition with alcohol; that we now seek to correct it under divine supervision.

The alcoholic must learn to "let go" whenever he becomes upset; when over-activity brings him feelings of mental and physical exhaustion; when he becomes extremely impatient; when he experiences anger; when he is bored; when he is resentful.

Relaxation will restore his sense of well-being and allow better concentration of his mental faculties which are necessary for an understanding of God sufficient to effect our recovery from alcoholism.

We regard the outcome of this step in complete confidence, as we know from the example of other members, that God's will can be understood; that our understanding of His care will give us new personalities that exclude alcohol—personalities that do happily relate us to God; to a conventional world and to our fellow men.

## STEP FOUR–*Made a searching and fearless moral inventory of ourselves*

———

The purpose of taking a moral inventory is to expose the noxious character traits of our alcoholic personalities, to eliminate them from the new personalities that with the help of the Alcoholics Anonymous Program as a "Way of Life," we now propose to develop.

The A.A. usage of the term "personality" deals with the development of new character traits necessary to our recovery from alcoholism. It has no relation to personal magnetism emanating from physical health, beauty or charm.

We gauge A.A. personality by A.A. maturity that is evidenced in such qualities as: Strength and understanding from a POWER GREATER THAN OURSELVES, surrender of self-centeredness, honesty, sincerity, practice of the Twelve Steps, creative thought, positive action in admitting wrongs and making amends, service to others and the example of a happy, sober life.

Before we can hope to develop the qualities that will create desirable A.A. personalities, we must discover the causes for our powerlessness over alcohol; we wish to know why we have been at war with ourselves; we propose to reveal and to study the limitations that alcoholism has placed upon our lives.

We hope to transcend our alcoholic limitations; to straighten out our unmanageable lives so we probe our alcoholic personalities—"To search out the flaws in our make-up which caused our failure."

The gravity of our drinking problem is deep-seated; it involves self-centered habits, emotions, moods, attitudes and misconceptions, which acquired over a period of years, have decreased our will power, weakened our physical resistance and have sponsored irrational thought and action. This has caused us extreme mental and physical hardship and brought anxiety and suffering to others.

Recovery from alcoholism is not possible until we have a knowledge of our defects, therefore we take definite steps toward correction of our physical, mental and spiritual disability when we make a searching and fearless moral inventory of ourselves; when we do it in a thorough businesslike way; when we reasonably excuse the other fellow and truly expose our own faults.

The beginner cannot fail to be impressed with the array of flaws he will uncover and will wish to correct. The caution to be observed in taking this step is that FEW OF US ARE READY AND WILLING TO SURRENDER *ALL* OF OUR DEFECTS.

# Step Four

We wish to cherish a few and by this procedure we encounter future trouble in the form of partial re-habilitation which is not the plan of the A.A. recovery program.

This step calls for a *complete inventory;* our program is not in accord with halfway measures or efforts; full rehabilitation is our objective. You defeat this purpose when you do not employ the inventory one hundred percent.

A moral inventory of a lifetime of drinking is not quickly recorded, nor is it a record that can be simply stated. We find in it many complexities that require study, and meditation. It must be honest, sincere and thorough. It must be a written inventory to be effective as it will later be checked against and often referred to. The mental self-appraisal is merely a supplement to the written inventory. It is necessary but not sufficient in itself.

Experience has taught us that this step should be started at once, but left open for future reference so that during the process of our mental and spiritual clean-up we can add the new items that will present themselves.

The brief discusison of a few imperfections permitted in this article is entirely inadequate to the thought and time you will need in applying this step to your alcoholic problem.

Reference to pages 64 to 71 inclusive in the Alcoholics Anonymous book will disclose a detailed discussion of Step Four. From these pages you will learn the manner in which our founders advocate that we work out our inventories.

You will discover that various manifestations of self-centeredness are undoubtedly the root of our trouble and that some of these manifestations present themselves in the form of RESENTMENT – DISHONESTY – SELF-PITY – JEALOUSY – CRITICISM – INTOLERANCE – FEAR – ANGER.

## *RESENTMENT*

Resentment is common to all alcoholics. We are never safe from it and as intangible as it may seem, it does pay off in material ways with destructive force and energy. Resentment is dynamite to the alcoholic.

In quoting the book, we are reminded that, "resentment is the NUMBER ONE OFFENDER. It destroys more alcoholics than anything else. From it stems all forms of spiritual disease, for we have not only been mentally and physically ill, we have been spiritually sick. When the spiritual malady is overcome, we straighten out mentally and physically.

"In dealing with resentments we set them on paper. We listed people, institutions and principals with whom we were angry. We asked ourselves why we were angry. In most cases we found that our self-esteem, our pocketbooks, our relationships (including sex), our ambitions were hurt or threatened. So we were sore; we were burnt up."

Make up your grudge list; see who you are inclosing in your circle of hatred; determine why you hold them there. Has your life been any happier because of this resentment? Were they really the offenders?

The founders of Alcoholics Anonymous answer the question with the definite statement: "It is plain that a life which includes deep resentment leads only to futility and unhappiness. To the precise extent that we permit these, do we squander the hours that might have been worth while."

They explain that resentment dwarfs the maintenance and growth of spiritual experience which is the only hope of the alcoholic and that without the sunlight of this experience the insanity of alcoholism returns and we drink again.

## *DISHONESTY*

"Those who do not recover through the help of our program are usually men and women who will not give themselves to the program and who are constitutionally incapable of being honest with themselves."

Dishonesty requires little further comment. It has no place in our program. It must be eliminated if we are to succeed at all.

Honesty with yourself, with God and your fellow man is the keystone in the A.A. bridge that spans the alcoholic chasm to permanent, happy sobriety.

Without honesty the Alcoholics Anonymous program would be a boring way of life. It would become inconsistent and cease to be constructive. The practice of dishonesty in any form helps to tear down the alcoholics defense against that first drink which he will eventually find himself taking, if he cannot be honest with himself.

## *CRITICISM*

Constructive criticism is truly a gesture of co-operation indicating a friendly interest that tends to improve conditions toward successful achievement of a common interest.

Well-meant criticism that is solicited can be most helpful and is encouraged because of its sincerity.

Negative criticism is absolutely out of our picture; it is a black sheep in the A.A. family and not conductive to healthy growth.

THE COMMON INTEREST OF THIS PRO-
GRAM IS SOBRIETY. Propriety in the use of
criticism is gauged by its good or bad influence in
helping either an individual or the whole group to
gain and maintain SOBRIETY.

Fault-finding and gossip will destroy the results
of much constructive A.A. effort. They serve no
good purpose so should be controlled with tolerance
and understanding, thus curbing our tendencies toward negative criticism.

If you must deal in criticism, confine your practice to self-criticism which is nothing more or less
than the object of this inventory.

### *SELF-PITY*

Self-pity is not generally regarded by alcoholics
as a particularly harmful emotion. We have all in-
dulged in varied forms of self-pity, the most common being that experience while enduring the tor-
tures of a hangover. Other forms of self-pity involve resentment and hatred brought on by real or
fancied wrongs, by acts of God, by ill luck or
disease.

Self-pity is often outright rebellion against circumstances of our own making where we feel sorry
for ourselves and assume a negative attitude toward
life.

It is not until we see in this emotion evidence of resentment and until we realize that it gives us the wrong attitude toward life and toward those we associate with, that we understand the necessity for its elimination.

The alcoholic must free himself from all forms of resentment; his happiness in life depends on his attitude and service toward others. He cannot afford to subject himself to self-pity because of its relationship to resentment and inferiority. It also retards his recovery from alcoholism by closing his mind to the wholesome, helpful opportunities about him and directs mental effort on self that should be centered in cooperative action with a Power Greater than Himself.

Experience has taught us that maturity in A.A. growth is stunted by self-pity. As we live and learn, we gain understanding of the value of stifling self-interest in our own miseries by taking to heart the problems of others.

The cure for self-pity is simple. It is within our reach: Look about you for somebody who has greater troubles than your own—help him in overcoming them. The benefits will be twofold and your problem will eliminate itself as you gain new strength in aiding a fellow sufferer to solve his troubles.

### *JEALOUSY*

Few, if any, men or women escape this emotional monstrosity. Its width and length are egotism and selfishness. Its depth is anger and resentment.

Jealousy of an individual's good standing, his personality, his talent or personal possessions can prey upon the human mind until, like a malignant disease, it injures or destroys it.

The beginner who takes the time to analyze jealousy finds in it a combination of all his pet imperfections. You are advised to make this analysis and thus acquaint yourself with its detailed cross section.

Strip off the harmless veneer so as to view the dangerous elements of its construction.

This cross section will reveal an astounding array of moral defects. They may appear in mild or passive form, yet they are all there: Self-pity–Resentment – Intolerance – Dishonesty – Cristicism – Anger – Hatred – Fear. It is also interesting to note that ignorance apparently bonds them all together.

It is well to avoid this compound emotion which can so easily jeopardize a member's mental fortitude and lead him into resentment and bitter hatred.

### INTOLERANCE

Lack of tolerance has much to do with that first drink, which under certain circumstances the alcoholic is unable to resist.

This condition existed when physical distress was experienced; when the realities of life became too demanding on our time and energy; when mental tension was great; when resentment at home or in business became unbearable; when business was poor; when, through over-activity, we became fatigued or were faced with other distracting circumstances. We felt that conditions had reached a breaking point; we became intolerant of them, so we got drunk.

It is well to remember the hardships we once suffered because of our intolerance and that some conditions will still seem intolerable even though we receive help from a Power Greater than Ourselves, but that the practice of tolerance gives us A.A. balance, conditions our character, and enables us to remain emotionally stable.

Evidence of intolerance in a member is not a good sign. It shows lack of equilibrium and indicates symptoms of an unstable mental and spiritual status. Our attitude of tolerance, where it should reasonably be expected, reflects our understanding and practice of the A.A. philosophy as a "Way of Life."

The alcoholic has consistently poached on the tolerance of mankind. He has much to amend in this respect, so should reverse his field at once by showing consideration where it is due.

We do not believe that tolerance of impossible situations makes good sense. God gave us intelligence to determine between good and bad, therefore, we find as much harm in being tolerant of wrong thought or action as we find in intolerance of the right things.

Discretion in the use of tolerance is necessary, but if we are practicing the A.A. program as a "Way of Life," we will find ourselves meeting the people half way of whom we have long been intolerant. Tolerance toward both new and old members who are sincerely trying to live this program is essential to our own recovery from alcoholism. If they are honestly trying to make A.A. their "Way of Life," we owe them our help.

It is not wise to become intolerant of conditions that you cannot change; the A.A. program advises you to gain an understanding of God's will. The condition that cannot be changed may be against the will of God. You should not view it with intolerance, but rather direct your time and energy in helpful, constructive activity where satisfactory results are possible.

"God grant us the serenity to accept the things we cannot change; courage to change the things we can, and wisdom to know the difference."

## *FEAR*

Fear is a specific emotion that is stimulated by many causes and impulses such as danger from without and anxiety from within. Anxiety and fear have a constructive place in the human mind so long as they are used for actual purposes of self-preservation and not carried beyond that point.

They can be employed to good advantage in A.A. if we understand them and cultivate their proper use.

All members should strive to cultivate an honest realistic evaluation of what alcohol does to them as insurance against the possibility of a return to drinking. We should be afraid to drink alcohol.

This is easily accomplished by a momentary mental picture of the helpless, unmanageable lives that alcohol demands from us. Intelligent use of this mental portrait in combating alcoholism is most helpful to permanent recovery. All successful members have utilized varied recollections of what alcoholism does to them as a preventive mental measure in overcoming urges or temptations that arise from temperament and environment.

The fact we have decided against drinking. that we have turned our lives over to God for help in our emergency does not guarantee the end of temptation. The human mind is susceptible to constant change. Temptation will enter it through devious channels. We have no knowledge of how or when the urge may come to us, but we can overcome it if we have prepared the right mental images and have fortified our minds with a knowledge of our alcoholic status and the fact that alcohol is no longer a beverage for us—it has become a poison.

Nature backs up this theory with dreams in which we find ourselves drinking. The remorse we suffer upon awakening is realistic; it leaves a lasting impression on our mind and furthers our determination to avoid future drinking.

Fear is too complex a subject to treat in this article; it had much to do with our drinking and undoubtedly has much to do with our recovery from alcoholism.

The member who finds that groundless fears constitute a menace to his sobriety should consult and receive treatment from an able psychiatrist.

Fear that does not constitute a malady can be corrected by the philosophy provided in our Alcoholics Anonymous program. Fear is nothing more or less than a distorted faith in the negative things of life and the evils *that might beset us*.

A.A. philosophy does not concern itself with anxiety over anything. As alcoholics we were once unstable with problems and anxieties that seemed impossible to remedy. The spiritual concepts of this program have removed them and have replaced them with peace of mind. We no longer worry; we have received a spiritual reprieve. This reprieve is extended from day to day by God in recognition for our appreciation of His help and the unselfish service we render to others.

Our antedote for fear is faith, not the distorted faith in fear, but rehabilitating all out faith in God, as we understand Him. We have found this to be an effective measure in overcoming all fears the alcoholic is subjected to.

*ANGER*

There is no single instance covered in the Twelve Steps where anger offers any benefit. We are led to believe, however, that it is a sort of mental poison that has the power to induce confused thinking and that under its sway we are more than apt to eventually resume the use of alcohol.

Anger is antagonistic to our philosophy. It

over-rides reason. Rehabilitation of an alcoholic "marks time" and progress stops so long as anger dominates. Various degrees of anger ranging from indignation to fury indicate diversified hazards to the member who makes his mind and actions subject to this strong emotion.

The following quotation from our A.A. book clearly predicts impending danger of those of us who allow ourselves to become bitterly provoked: "If we were to live we had to be free from anger. The grouch and the brainstorm were not for us. They may be the dubious luxury of normal men, but for alcoholics these things are poison."

A simple analysis of this emotion should cure our further indulgence. In it the impulse to injure either friend or enemy is always present. When fully aroused this impulse is often sufficient to cause murder.

The beginner is only human. He will be subject to all human impulses and often faced by conditions that arouse him, but he need not be ignorant of the treacherous nature of anger or the insidious inroads its impulses can effect upon his recovery.

In compiling our inventories let us keep in mind the fact that we are alcoholics; that we are sick physically, mentally and spiritually; that we have been unable to recover from our illness through our own efforts, but that thousands of alcoholics before us have effected their recovery by exchanging their alcoholic personalities for the happy, sober personalities brought about by the A.A. way of living. With this in mind, we call upon a POWER GREATER THAN OURSELVES to help guide us in making a searching and fearless moral inventory of ourselves as one of the steps necessary for our recovery.

## STEP FIVE—*Admitted to God, to ourselves and to another human being the exact nature of our wrongs*

---

If we have been honest and thorough with our personal inventory we have listed and analyzed our resentments and have a record of the harm we have caused others.

We have a list of our grosser handicaps and imperfections and also the names of the people who have suffered as a result of our unmanageable lives and insane behavior.

These facts indicate certain defects in our lives; they constitute the record we have made of our wrongs. We have ascertained our weak spots and not only propose to erase them, but also to prepare a plan of action that will bring restitution and happiness to the men and women who have suffered mental, physical or financial harm as a direct result of our uncontrolled drinking.

Step Five is a preparatory step to the restitution that we expect to make as we carry out the provision of Step Nine, where amends are necessary and we make them.

The exact nature of our wrongs must be admitted to God and ourselves and then talked over with a *third person*.

The general trend of thought with the new member is to discount the importance of admitting anything to ANOTHER HUMAN BEING.

The founders of our movement knew the value of doing this; they knew that only by so doing could we acquire the humility and spiritual inspiration necessary to continuous development in A.A. philosophy.

Most of us felt that our self appraisals were exacting and because we had conceded to God the error of our former alcoholic thought and conduct we saw no need to go farther. We reasoned that God knew; that He would forgive us and so the matter was closed.

This is sugar-coated alcoholic thinking. It follows the old pattern and is but a pretense, a new form of escape from responsibility. We must give our long hoarded secrets to another person if we are to gain peace of mind, confidence and self respect.

The humility this step brings us is imperative to our future welfare. We will have no spiritual inspiration, no release from anxiety and fear until we remove the skeleton from our closet. We are to stop dodging people and start facing facts and issues, if freedom from dread and tension is to be ours.

# STEP FIVE

Step Five is a pivotal step. It calls for action that starts a real spiritual awakening as we back up our FAITH with VERBAL WORKS.

If this step seems difficult to you, (and it may well seem that way) remember that you are no exception. Many of us experienced the same reaction. This reaction is nothing more than the reflexes of a dying alcoholic instinct trying to avoid reality—too little time has elapsed between our sudden change from an alcoholic's rationalization to that of rehabilitative conduct necessary to our program. We unconsciously are being dominated by our old thoughts. These are but momentary thoughts of rebellion. They will quickly give way to the sublimating power of our new philosophy if we will be open-minded and have faith that God will aid us in arriving at the right solution.

The step specifically outlines the action to be taken. When the right time arrives, arrange an interview with any one outside of A.A. who will be *understanding but unaffected* by your narration. We must avoid people who will let out facts harmful to others. For this reason a stranger is our best bet—the doctor, lawyer, psychiatrist, priest, or minister. Any of these will serve our purpose. Most men of the callings mentioned are qualified and will be honored by the confidence placed in them when they hear our story.

There is no stated time for taking this step—it is not to be rushed into. We do not take it as a form that must be complied with. There is a state of mind that will arise in all sincere members who "lose themselves" in A.A. philosophy which will indicate clearly when they are ready. When this time arrives, however, we must act at once. To purposely postpone it is inconsistent to our plan of recovery.

You are now engaged in a business deal with God and another human being. If your inventory has been thorough, "You are in a position to pocket your pride," to tell a story "that will illuminate every twist of character, every dark cranny of the past." You have no reason to doubt the psychological and spiritual value offered. You will be well rewarded for your effort and will find yourself at a loss to express in words the gratification that will be yours. *Understanding of such things comes only with EXPERIENCE.*

Interpretation of the deep significance of admitting our wrongs to God, ourselves and another human being are logically summed up by saying, "Once we have taken this step, withholding nothing, we are delighted. We can look the world in the eye. We begin to feel the nearness of our Creator. *We have had* certain spiritual beliefs, but *NOW WE BEGIN TO HAVE A SPIRITUAL EXPERI-ENCE.*"

The metamorphosis from the alcoholic to the NEW A.A. PERSONALITY shows its first sign of life upon completion of Step Five. We are impressed with the simplicity of this effective spiritual device which has been the means of starting within us a spiritual awakening. The step is a direct challenge to our sincerity, inasmuch as we have been promised humility and a spiritual experience when we have talked over our defects with a third person.

This is the one step in the program that advises you what to do when you have completed it. This advice is given in our A.A. book. It says, "Returning home we find a place where we can be quiet for an hour, carefully reviewing what we have done. We thank God from the bottom of our hearts that we know HIM better. Taking this book down from our shelf we turn to the page which contains the Twelve Steps. Carefully reading the first five proposals we ask if we have omitted anything, for we are building AN ARCH THROUGH WHICH WE WILL WALK A FREE MAN AT LAST. Is our work solid so far? Are the stones properly in place? Have we skimped on the cement put into the foundation? Have we tried to make mortar without sand? If we can answer to our satisfaction, we can then look to Step Six."

STEP SIX—*We were entirely ready to have God remove all these defects of character*

STEP SEVEN—*Humbly ask Him to remove our shortcomings*

———

It is only after we have completed Step Five, when humility has been experienced and self-respect has been restored, as a result of our admitting to God and to another human being the exact nature of our wrongs, that we are in a suitable spiritual condition to sincerely carry out the provisions of Steps Six and Seven.

This action brings a heretofore unknown feeling of moral strength. For the first time we are facing our REAL SELVES—the selves whose withered roots have touched and are now drawing upon an unfailing source of assurance, power and security.

We find in the consummation of these steps a NEW PEACE, a release from TENSION and ANXIETY as we now are laying our misconceptions, our defects of character in God's hands. We are asking Him to rid them from our lives. We are exerting great mental cooperation with God. We feel an intense humility that cries out for recognition and Divine Help.

The SPIRITUAL LIFT, the nearness to our CREATOR that is experienced from humble invocation of HIS help and our willingness to be freed from old willful thoughts and habits are all essential to successful attainment of these steps.

The mental hygiene and spiritual housecleaning we have started in our inventories and continued in Step Five, reaches its climax in Step Seven when we fully subject our wills to God and wish to surrender to HIM all of our moral imperfections.

The several objectives of Steps Six and Seven are:

1. To gain an intimate contact with this POWER GREATER THAN OURSELVES.
2. To perfect ourselves in the practice of unselfish prayer.
3. To be aware of our defective character traits.
4. To desire their removal.
5. Complete surrender of all defects of character.
6. To believe that God CAN remove them.
7. To ask Him to take them *ALL AWAY*.

The results we expect from pursuit of these objectives are:

1. A reconciliation to God's way of doing business. We become "fed up" with our way and

with further practice of our defective character traits.

2. A willingness to work out a plan for suppression of self-centeredness through gaining a conscious contact with God.

3. To experience dissatisfaction and remorse as a result of our alcoholic practices and to seek a spiritual inspiration that will bring us an inner sense of poise and security.

4. Increased faith, clean hearts and minds, ability to offer unselfish prayer.

5. A spiritual courage that is fearless in its outlook on life; a desire to make restitution to those our drinking has harmed.

6. A desire to quit bluffing and honestly give God a chance to remove from our lives all that stands in the way of our usefulness to Him, and to others.

7. Elimination of our defective character traits, acquisition of humility.

The spiritual attitude and satisfactory frame of mind necessary to effective fulfillment of these steps has been progressively worked toward in the completion of the first five steps in our program.

Knowledge of our alcoholic problem prompts us to turn to God for help. The alcoholic must pray. There is no standard form of prayer to use. Our remorse over past mistakes and a genuine desire to correct them will indicate how we shall pray.

We all come before God as offenders. We offer no alibis. We have no defense. We stand before him subject to the weaknesses of alcoholism. We ask for an understanding of this disease and for HIS strength and help in combatting it. We wish to arrest it but only for unselfish purposes. We ask forgiveness for the sins we have committed. We ask for protection from self-pity, from resentments, from all selfishness. We ask for wisdom and understanding to know HIS will. We ask for spiritual and physical strength to execute His will. WE ask HIM to keep us willing to follow the A.A. program. WE thank HIM for the help it has given us and others. WE ask HIM to credit its founders with this help. We acknowledge our many shortcomings. *WE HUMBLY ASK HIM TO REMOVE THEM.*

There is nothing outstanding about an alcoholic's prayer to God. It is just a simple, sincere affair in which the alcoholic has nothing to lose but from which he gains SOBRIETY–SANE THOUGHT AND BEHAVIOR–PEACE OF MIND–A N D HAPPINESS FOR HIMSELF AND FAMILY.

There is a latent power within each human being that responds to conscious contact with God. This contact, if honest and unselfish, generates a stable, balanced strength that surmounts seemingly impos-

sible circumstances. THROUGH IT, THE MIR-
ACLE OF A.A. IS POSSIBLE.

Steps Six and Seven utilize this contact which
thousands of alcoholics have humbly used in effecting removal of their defects of character.

In these two steps are found the forge in which
we heat the separate links that go into the new personality chains we are building. *Without them our
rehabilitation is impossible.*

STEP EIGHT–*Made a list of all the people we had harmed and become willing to make amends to them all*

STEP NINE–*Made direct amends to such people wherever possible, except when to do so would injure them or others*

––––––

The objective of Steps Eight and Nine is to *outline* and put into *practice* a working course of conduct which will directly rectify the harm or injury our drinking may have imposed upon others; at the same time start harmoniously relating us to life and to our fellow men.

The practice of the Alcoholics Anonymous philosophy adequately fulfills these requirements. It is a PROVEN WAY OF LIFE by which the alcoholic corrects his past mistakes and makes restitution to relative, friend or enemy as he effects his own recovery from the physical and mental damage alcohol has inflicted upon him.

Many alcoholics have agreed to the effectiveness of our philosophy but have failed to benefit from it because they take too lightly the seriousness of this physical and mental damage and do not wish to inconvenience themselves with the provisions of our program. They also find it difficult to understand that they are spiritual invalids.

Members do not arrest alcoholism or gain recovery by merely agreeing with the principles of A.A. philosophy—THEY RECOVER *ONLY IF THEY LIVE THEM*.

These steps work in conjunction with each other. We have a list of those we have harmed—we have our grudge list—we have a list of those we are financially obligated to. FEW of us realize that our own names head the list of those we have wronged and that by living this program we are first making amends to ourselves—to our outraged constitutions—to our confused minds and to our troubled spirits.

It is not a difficult thing to list the people who suffered because we drank. Our real problem is to arrive at a state of mind that concedes the damage we have done and embraces a sincere willingness to amend it.

Step Nine is not easily or quickly carried out. Some restitution is started upon our acceptance of the A.A. program as a "Way of Life." This is usually quite limited as it is not until we have spent several months in A.A. and have fortified our sobriety with good fundamental knowledge of the program that we acquire the spiritual courage and understanding to discreetly dispense reparation.

The member is confronted with many obstacles in observance of this step. We find procrastination a hindrance to some members. This should be avoided. On the other hand, there are those who are too ambitious to rebuild; to get the thing over with at once. Remember, that in most cases you will require a lifetime to complete Step Nine. Some members under inspiration of the new personalities they are creating become emotional and act on the spur of the moment. Their hasty action is apt to fall short of accomplishment. Pride is another barrier. Confusion, through improper interpretation of the purpose of this step, is a common handicap.

The older members will be helpful, if consulted, wherever perplexities are encountered. Do not act hastily or in doubt—invite their opinions—then formulate a plan of action with God and start making right the wrongs for which you are responsible.

Meditation and prayer are necessary in order to make amends. No amend should be made that is not preceded by prayer as it will lack complete purpose and effectiveness. Conscious contact with God in the matter of making amends will not only bring about a more satisfactory result, but will also aid you in determining those amends to avoid which might injure others. Discretion in this connection is imperative.

God's presence in our lives now alters and sublimates our mental and physical activities. It gives us the humility we need to make amends and an incentive to get started. "WE ARE TRYING TO PUT OUR LIVES IN ORDER. WE DO THIS THROUGH MAXIMUM SERVICE TO GOD AND THE PEOPLE ABOUT US."

The question now arises: Whose names belong on our list? How do we go about it in making amends to these people? What procedure do we follow?

Our answers to these questions are found in the Alcoholics Anonymous book on pages 76 to 84, inclusive.

The following summary of certain advice taken from those pages is incomplete and must be enlarged upon by each member in application to his particular needs.

We find it impossible to cover this complex matter in its entirety, but have listed a few suggestions and examples for guidance. Our list classifies four types of people and comments on a fifth who is not generally included in the list to whom amends are made, yet who must constantly be considered, if permanent sobriety is to be assured.

### *GROUP ONE–FRIENDS*

In this group are the people who have been close friends, business associates, etc., those toward whom we should be friendly, but have severed connections with because of resentments, pride or fancied wrongs. The ones we have treated unjustly, but have not harmed aside from harsh words or acts of asinine behavior, where indebtedness is not a consideration.

The technique to be observed in approaching the people in this class is based on sincerity. Our approach is "calm, frank and open." We aim to convince the party of our good intentions and to assure him that we regret the treatment he has received at our hands.

We explain our alcoholic illness, the nature of resentments and hatred in relation to our sobriety. We outline our good intentions and ask forgiveness and cooperation in our future associations. Our purpose is to create good will and regain friendship.

We avoid impressing anyone with the idea that we are religious fanatics, but we never sidestep the spiritual issue or deny God if He is brought into the conversation.

We do not attempt amends to those "who are

still smarting from a recent injustice" and never make any amends that will harm another person.

There will be few cases where our advances are rejected. If we are unable to establish a reconciliation and are not favorably received, we simply drop the matter in hopes that eventually our sobriety and future dealings will repair the breach between us.

The main point to keep in mind is that we are out to perform a duty, that we will not be upset or discouraged by gruff or unpleasant receptions, that the intent of our visit is a harmonious one and that UNDER NO CONSIDERATION WILL WE LEAVE IN AN ANGRY OR RESENTFUL MOOD.

## *GROUP TWO–FAMILIES*

The people under this group are generally found in our families. The outstanding examples are the wives of the alcoholic, or in the case of the alcoholic women, the husbands. Then follow the mothers, fathers, sons, daughters, and often close friends whose lives we have "kept in turmoil because of our selfish and inconsiderate habits." We have been "like a tornado roaring our way through the lives of others," breaking hearts and "killing sweet relationships." The damage we have done to this group has been spread over many years. It will take many years to undo it.

Our approach technique is no problem here, unless homes have been broken up and separation makes reparation contacts impossible. Even then, the member will benefit from living the program, as his record of sobriety usually comes to the attention of the injured one. Time may be required to effect reconciliation, but satisfactory adjustments are generally forthcoming. Often this has been handled through correspondence. Direct contact is preferable in all cases wherever possible.

If the home is still intact the member's family is aware of his desire to treat his alcoholic illness and seldom fails to back him up in this purpose.

It is important that they read the book, "Alcoholics Anonymous," to gain an understanding of alcoholism and the steps outlined in our program for its treatment. A new members needs the full understanding and cooperation of his family. His amends to them are most thorough and are made with greater ease when they realize what he is trying to do.

Sobriety for us is a blessing to the individuals

in Group Two. As a rule, it is the greatest single amend we can make them, yet it is a partial amend that must be followed up with kind and thoughtful acts. Sobriety in itself is not enough. We must be attentive and considerate of the family as a whole. Harmony and cooperation must be established. Evidence of our love and a desire to become worthy of their respect will be most helpful. Irreparable damage is not unusual. When encountered it can only be offset by obvious manifestation of our willingness to right the condition if it were possible. We lose no time in making the amends that are possible.

Sex problems complicate the lives of many alcoholics. The first consideration in handling them is to stop the trouble at its source. Honesty is a prime factor in the lives of all members and leaves no room for adultery.

Injury to others must be considered in straightening out our sex problems. We always use great tact in handling the situation if amends are in order. Jealousy, when aroused, greatly impedes our progress. Fairness, meditation and prayer must be relied upon. We lay the matter in God's hands and are then guided by the dictates of His inspiration and will.

## GROUP THREE–CREDITORS

"We do not dodge our creditors." The creditor usually knows about our drinking. If not, we should "lay our cards on the table." If payment is impossible, arrange the best deal we can. It may be a future date when we will start paying or possibly we can pay even small amounts until we become financially able to increase them. The main idea is *to have an UNDERSTANDING*. We must be at ease in this connection, otherwise fear may return us to drinking. When the creditor understands the nature of our alcoholic illness he will readily see that money cannot be forthcoming unless we maintain sobriety and thus be in a better mood to receive our proposition.

## GROUP FOUR–THE DECEASED

The harm we have done to departed relatives or friends is often a cause for self-condemnation. This should not be; it is a harmful practice that is unwise because there is no remedy for it.

We must realize the futility of remorse over wrongs that we cannot amend. We do not allow such errors of the past to impair our future usefulness. We reason that the harm done would be partly offset by the new philosophy we are living.

That inasmuch as we cannot reach the departed one we can still make amends to living relatives. If this is impossible we resort to God in prayer, asking Him to see the willingness in our hearts and to forgive us in connection with these people.

Then there are *the amends we must daily make to God*. These become automatic; they are the requirements of each of the Twelve Steps. The A.A. program is ONE BIG AMEND broken up into twelve parts.

Before we can settle for the harm done others we must eliminate the source of moral and physical devastation to ourselves.

Alcoholism is our disease. It accounts for the imposition of injury upon our families and friends; upon those loved ones who have departed. It accounts for our indebtedness; it is responsible for our impaired physical condition; it has brought us irrational thinking, insane behavior, spiritual illness.

We make amends to ourselves, to the personalities we were before becoming alcoholic, by understanding our disease, by illuminating our defects of character, by eliminating them from our lives, by intelligent physical care of our bodies, by restoration of our mental apparatus through sobriety, by treatment of our spiritual illness through recourse to understanding and practice of God's Will. The alcoholic's rehabilitation is contingent upon amends and will be *SO LONG AS HE LIVES*.

We often are inclined to clutter up our list with petty wrongs long forgotten and of no great importance. Amends of this sort would never end; they should be forgotten. Many of us have been uncertain over the advisability of making some amends. The yardstick to use in this connection is your conscience; if the wrong bothers you it should undoubtedly be amended.

The people covered in this discussion will not comprise a full list of those we make amends to. There will be others on our list and we will find that new errors constantly occurring in our lives will send us back to make reparation to those already on the list.

Step Nine has reclaimed many broken friendships; it has brought peace and happiness to the lives of those who suffered because of our alcoholism. Its great rehabilitative power has also affected the lives of thousands of alcoholics through the spiritual awakening they have experienced. Because of this step, these same alcoholics have recovered their self-respect, they have taken on courage and confidence, they have assumed responsibility. They sense God's presence and with His presence comes the realization that their lives are again manageable.

STEP TEN—*Continued to take personal inventory and when we were wrong promptly admitted it*

————

Step Ten is one of the maintenance steps. Its purpose is to remind us that the moral defects we have recognized in selfishness, dishonesty, resentment, and fear are still problems we daily encounter; that they remain a handicap to normal, happy living; that we should set up a perpetual inventory to guard against them; that we continue to freely admit our wrongs.

George A. Dorsey contributes a bit of interesting information relative to the instability of man's nature by saying, "Man is something happening all the time; he is a going concern, he makes his rules, revises his formulae and recasts his mould in the act of being and while going. IT IS IN MAN'S NATURE THAT HE DOES NOT STAY PUT."

The value of a perpetual inventory is to keep us from GOING STALE. It helps us to STAY PUT.

Through it we avoid the unhappy experiences that follow when we are dominated by forms of self-centeredness which try to creep back into our lives.

We make the inventory a sort of intelligence department that identifies moral defects both old and new. It is a Rogue's Gallery where we catalogue each defect and its alias so when self-centeredness, for instance, disguises itself in the form of complacency or boredom, we detect the deception and arrest it.

These defects are great sources of danger to us. They had much to do with the grief we once suffered from abnormal drinking. They can still return us to the Insanity of Alcoholism.

Step Four provided us with an inventory that served a definite purpose. It exposed character defects we formerly refused to recognize—defects that obstructed successful living. The necessity of knowing these faults is quite clear now but was not so obvious at the time our inventory was taken.

The inventory supplied us with an understanding of our problem. It brought us face to face with ourselves—to our shortcomings—to the sense of removing them with God's help. It was indispensable at the time but fulfilled its intended use once the nature of our self-willed alcoholic habit and defects were recorded. Without this record, progress in A.A. would have been impossible.

Because of this record, progress has been made. Knowledge of our moral defects and practice of the A.A. program have completely changed our lives, our attitude toward our own problems and our feeling toward our fellow men.

We have gained the confidence and the respect of others. Many of our friends have expressed their admiration of the sobriety we have acquired. Pride and satisfaction naturally follow this accomplishment. We enjoy our security and the friendly attitude of those about us.

Step Ten will safeguard this progress if we continue our personal inventories and promptly admit it when we are wrong.

Let us not forget, however, that alcoholics never seem to stay put. Our founders knew this from their own experiences. They knew that drinking habits of long standing would cry aloud for customary performance privileges.

They knew that new character defects would appear and that many of the old ones would present themselves in disguised form. Hence the perpetual inventory to announce the advent of each old habit and a sort of mental sentry on guard to detect the new ones.

Interpretation of Step Ten does not allow us to accept the inventory taken in Step Four as complete or final.

The reason for this is apparent when we consider our natural inclination to regard the complete record of wrongs as those we listed in Step Four. It is true that this list covered our wrongs of that date, but we deceive ourselves when we make no allowance for the additional weaknesses developed in the meanwhile.

The plan of our philosophy is to *live each step*. The object of Step Ten is not only to continue our personal inventory, but also to check daily the progress we are making with each step in the A.A. program.

By reviewing them we often find ourselves "off the beam." This is a bad spot for an alcoholic who invariably goes whole hog if immediate steps toward correction are not taken.

Correction is possible if we realize our danger when our inventories reveal it to us. Prompt action upon such discovery is necessary. It is not unusual to find ourselves off the beam—the idea is to get back on again. The inventory is essential to this requirement.

So that the new member may recognize a few of the "off the beam" positions it may be well to list them:

1.  When you have forgotten that you are an alcoholic—that you have a nervous system which is incapable of withstanding the "soothing influence" of alcohol.

2.  When complacency lowers your guard and

allows resentment and intolerance to creep back into your life.

3. When you begin pulling A.A. boners and remain human enough to overlook them.

4. When you become cocky over your A.A. success and cease contact with God.

5. When you lack interest in new members and feel it inconvenient to help them.

6. When you become irked with meetings and peevish with other members.

7. When boredom makes an appearance.

8. Traveling without the A.A. book.

When the inventory discloses that you show any of these symptoms you may be sure that one of your outstanding troubles is self-centeredness. Further investigation will unearth a severe case of spiritual constipation.

The antidote for these troubles is to apply yourself to a close study of our program. Read the book. Talk A.A. with the members. Sincerely interest yourself in your A.A. group. Attend more meetings. Do your bit. Put your shoulder to the wheel. Get busy. Lose yourself in the program. Work with new members. Review the miracle that God has performed in your life. Be honest and thankfully offer a prayer of appreciation. Always carry the A.A. book on out of town trips.

The second part of Step Ten, "WHEN WE WERE WRONG, PROMPTLY ADMITTED IT," is not to be taken lightly. It is a good character conditioner. Recognition of a wrong is not enough; verbal acknowledgement should follow. The requirements of our program are to make amends, if the wrong has harmed anyone. The inventory keeps us alert to our responsibility in this matter.

The ambitious member will apply these things to himself. He will search out the significance of "Admitting It When He Is Wrong."

Do you remember in Step Five when we admitted to God, to ourselves, and to another human being the exact nature of our wrongs? How we meditated our shortcomings in Steps Six and Seven? How vital it was to our well-being at the time?

It is still vital. We haven't changed in that respect and we never will. Alcoholism has been arrested, but we have not been cured.

It is not in the nature of the alcoholic to stay put. He must admit his wrongs to receive the feeling of nobility and exaltation that keeps him in the right mental and spiritual condition to maintain contented, permanent sobriety.

Continue this inventory daily. When you are wrong understand the value of getting it off your chest at once. Don't be afraid to admit your mistakes. Remember, that any fool can defend his errors. Get out of that class. Remember that your

NEW PERSONALITY IS NOT COMPATIBLE WITH MORAL DEFECTS OR CONCEALED ERRORS.

Step Ten is practical not only in our philosophy, but for daily living as well.

Observation and practice of this step keeps us alert. It creates a stable, balanced mental and spiritual condition.

It makes us more self-critical and less apt to criticize others. It keeps us on the beam.

Check yourself thoroughly. Don't make a farce of your life. You owe it to God, yourself and your family to make real headway. You must THINK SOBER and LIVE SOBER.

The inventory will help you to know just what degree of success you are attaining in A.A. It will let you know where you stand. It will keep you in GOOD STANDING.

STEP ELEVEN—*Sought through prayer and meditation to improve our conscious contact with God as we understood Him, praying only for knowledge of His will for us and the power to carry that out*

———

This step can be broken down into three parts. Let us first consider that part which recommends the need for prayer and meditation to improve our understanding of God, our contact with Him.

A prayer for improved contact with God, for knowledge of His will, and for mental, physical and spiritual energy to carry it out, requires the co-ordinated effort of all our faculties.

Knowledge of the need of this step is based on the past experience of A.A. members, *some of whom have demonstrated the ability to forget that they HAVE NOT been CURED OF ALCOHOLISM.* They have mistaken recovery for cure, so after a few months of sobriety have considered practice of the A.A. philosophy unnecessary. They have overlooked the fact that the human mind was not constituted to remember the pain and sorrow suffered from disease. They take their changed personalities TOO MUCH FOR GRANTED, assuming that once acquired they will always stay with them.

God's help was needed in their dire emergency, but that is passed now. They say, "We will never drink again, we never even think about it." They let down their guard and ease up on spiritual contacts and service.

A positive attitude toward permanent sobriety is commendable. It is the attitude we wish all members to take.

The fact we have no desire or intention to ever drink again is a favorable frame of mind for the new member to hold. It is our ambition, a mental condition to be grateful for, BUT ONE THAT TOO OFTEN FOSTERS COMPLACENCY WHICH CAN LEAD US INTO TROUBLE UNLESS GOD IS GIVEN FULL CREDIT FOR THE SOBRIETY WE ENJOY.

When complacency develops we are apt to forget the part that God has played in effecting our rehabilitation. We overlook the fact that our nervous systems are still those of alcoholics. We seem to forget that as alcoholics we are susceptible to moods and emotions that we formerly appeased with alcohol. Complacency obscures the knowledge that our recovery from alcoholism was granted by a POWER GREATER THAN OURSELVES, that without contact with God, reversion to our old low physical and spiritual levels is probable.

Cooperation with a POWER GREATER THAN OURSELVES has pulled us out of the alcoholic rut.

Step Eleven is a maintenance step that was planned to keep us out and to make us stay put.

It keeps us spiritually active and in tune with God. It insures against the dulling of inspiration as our alcoholic problems diminish.

Understanding of this situation and the knowledge that members do get "off the beam" spiritually at times, is our first line of defense. We fortify this defense by keeping uppermost in our minds that "In reality we are on a DAILY REPRIEVE, that our reprieves are CONTINGENT UPON OUR SPIRITUAL CONDITION."

The bitter experiences of members who insist upon learning the hard way—the backsliders who returned to drinking—attest to the truth of this statement.

Invariably their trouble FIRST STARTS WITH NEGLECT OF PRAYER and matures when they completely abandon conscious contact with God and service to others.

Our realization of God's help in the past impresses us with the fact that it can be utilized to even better use in the future. A sure way of increasing this help and expanding our contact with God is possible through simple prayers of sincere appreciation. Meditate on the help He has given, acknowledge its source, be genuine in your thanks for HIS understanding of your alcoholic problem and the strength HE has given you to overcome it.

He has demonstrated a miracle in our lives, so our problem no longer is entirely one of achievement. We have acquired sobriety and are enjoying its benefits. Through it we have regained health, mentality and have built up self-respect within ourselves, at home and among our friends. It is our privilege and duty to safeguard and protect this miracle. It was accomplished through humility, faith and prayer as we actively tried to understand and carry out HIS will.

Prayers of appreciation are not all that we indulge in, but they are unselfish and are the quickest means of bringing us into HIS presence. Contacting God with thanks and appreciation will supply fast inspiration that goes a long way toward improving our understanding and nearness to Him. Such contacts renew our faith and keep us active.

Each member will naturally have his own technique in improving his contact with God, but if actual prayers of appreciation are missing, the technique should be enlarged to include them. It is more sensible to ask for a required circumstance after you have acknowledged and expressed thanks for receiving a previous one.

Prayer and meditation to improve our conscious

contact with God seem easiest when we are relaxed and composed, when strife, fear and resentment are laid aside and we are in harmony with those about us. For this reason it is advisable to consider the importance of mental composure and physical relaxation insofar as prayer is concerned, and to further comment upon them as stabilizers to the restless nature of the alcoholic.

The point in mind is that the Twelve Steps will lead many of us to recognize our need for spiritual help, but will not direct attention to the fact we may be abusing our source of physical and mental energy.

Relaxation of mind and body and surrender of our will to God are undoubtedly necessary before satisfactory prayer and meditation are engaged in.

We owe God both humility and respect; we show it by freeing ourselves, for the moment, from material consideration, from self-pity, fear or anxiety, and by giving Him our undivided attention.

It is profitable for us to understand the value of keeping our bodies in a healthy condition, to practice poise and composure.

The alcoholic is apt to possess a restless disposition that tends toward over-activity. He not only practiced this by uncontrolled drinking, but showed evidence of his intemperance in many other ways.

By reason of this fact we recommend relaxation as an aid to prayer and suggest that a quiet time, aside from prayer, will be beneficial to all alcoholics.

The habit of relaxation practiced during quiet times at intervals throughout each day, is exactly what we need. Prominent medical authorities agree on this matter.

The intervals will be determined by our moods and mental attitudes, by our response to fear, anger, fatigue, emotional stress, or whenever we feel the pressure of high nerve tension.

The ill effects of these things upon the alcoholic's mental condition decidedly regulate his behavior. They constitute a hazard that jeopardizes his chances of recovery.

These are the things he once relieved by drinking. He cannot ignore them now, and expect to function normally or attain that degree of spiritual or mental efficiency which composure would bring.

How do we do this? We attempt to momentarily suspend all mental and physical activities. We try to relax our entire bodies, then close our minds to the worries and anxieties about us.

What do we think about? Nothing, let go of everything, just rest and learn to "TAKE IT EASY."

How long do we continue this? Be your own judge. It can be a matter of minutes if necessary. We know, however, from experience, that even 30 *SECONDS OF COMPLETE RELAXATION* of mind and body will do the trick. It is a simple trick. Try it.

You owe it to yourself and to the people about you. Your conscious contact with God is hardly complete without it.

The second part of this step deals with PRAYER FOR A KNOWLEDGE OF HIS WILL. This knowledge will bring the proper use of our will, which seems to be tied up in self-denial and willing service to others.

The question that has repeatedly confronted members is—WHAT IS GOD'S WILL?—HOW AM I TO KNOW IT FROM MY OWN WILL?

We do not attempt to directly answer this question. It is not our responsibility. It is the duty of the church and organized religion to interpret God's will.

As members of Alcoholics Anonymous we can use the intelligence HE gave, however, and through deduction arrive at our understanding of HIS will for us in A.A. Through contemplation of the matter in this respect we offer the following explanation.

The will of God would not be difficult of execution if there was no one but yourself in this world to consider.

You would not lie to yourself as you do under the present circumstances; cheating would not only be unnecessary, it would be impossible. You could hardly commit adultery and there would be no excuse or occasion for leading a double life.

Drunkenness under such circumstances would not harm anyone but yourself. Moral values would be entirely changed, making sin impossible, unless you denied God completely. The nature of our prayers would have little resemblance to the prayers we now offer. The chief need we would have for God then would be that of personal contact to offset loneliness, to avert danger, to cure sickness and to establish security in the world hereafter.

We, therefore, deduct that our understanding of God's will IS TO BE FOUND IN OUR ATTITUDE TOWARDS OUR FELLOW MEN AND IN THE TREATMENT WE ACCORD THEM. "We cannot live unto ourselves alone."

The worth-while spiritual experience all of us have had really came after we had renounced self-will and were admitting our wrongs, making amends, or performing charitable deeds that benefited others at the expense of our time and money.

It was only while engaged in thought and activity of this nature that we keenly felt the presence of God, or came close to the knowledge of HIS will. The answer to our prayer for such understanding comes with the least effort when we are busy on spiritual missions of help and service to our families, to our friends, or when we are at work with new members. Our efforts in this direction, aided by faith and prayer for guidance have brought us near to God.

Daily practice of the Alcoholics Anonymous program keeps us close to the spiritual and physical needs of humanity. There is much work to be done in its rehabilitation, as we interest ourselves in this work and carry it on, WE ARE, TO THE BEST OF OUR ABILITY AND KNOWLEDGE, GAINING AN UNDERSTANDING OF G O D ' S WILL THROUGH THE S E R V I C E WE RENDER OTHERS.

The active member who is trying to carry the will of God into his daily life should never become discouraged when he is criticised at home, or by fellow members of the organization, *so long as his motives are sincere and constructive*. If he is wrong, he admits it and seeks further understanding from God. He keeps on trying. Faith in his work and prayer must be maintained.

Appreciation of this situation is necessary by all members. None of us should question the works of another *unless we know the motive behind them is foreign to God's will*.

Criticism, even when in order, should be of a constructive nature. When offered it should be of co-operative intent, not the result of resentment or envy.

The older members make moves or advocate policies that are generally sound and wise as they base them on understanding of past experiences. The newer man may question them and through lack of understanding take a fixed stand against their adoption.

We are, therefore, cautioned against questioning the acts of any member until we know his motive, until we know he is wrong. If he is right we could easily be questioning the will of God. Our purpose is to conform to it, NEVER TO OPPOSE IT.

The third part of this step relates to prayer for the power to CARRY OUT GOD'S WILL. This prayer is for MENTAL EFFICIENCY, FOR SPIRITUAL STRENGTH and for PHYSICAL INDURANCE.

We must merit the power we seek by first improving our efficiency. Mental energy, spiritual strength, and physical endurance are not granted until we qualify for them. We may pray for them, and we should, but they cannot be had for the asking alone. They must be earned by honest endeavor.

This power is developed as we surrender self-centeredness and with consideration, tolerance and humility take over the supervision of another person's problems.

We cannot live his life for him, but we can help him to help himself. Our interest will supply the incentive to urge him on to renewed effort. Our concern over his program will enrich our own resourcefulness as we devise ways and means for his recovery. As we help him develop his strength we will unconsciously be gaining power and strength ourselves.

It is not wise to pray for power selfishly or with resentment, envy or self-pity in our hearts. This prayer is never granted. A.A. philosophy is not planned along such lines. We never expect results until we have overcome our defects and have things under control. When this has been accomplished we not only pray for the right results, but fully believe they will be granted.

At times we seem to forget our "Way of Life" and try to force issues. We mistake our own wilfullness for Divine Will and by sheer will power accomplish certain objectives. The true source of such power soon becomes evident. We find ourselves out of harmony with other members, we fail to sense that warm feeling of satisfaction, we lack proper inspiration. We are unappreciated and misunderstood. We are doing things from which we derive no pleasure and which are not particularly useful to others. When this occurs we may be sure that the power we are generating has no connection with the POWER GREATER THAN OURSELVES.

It is safe to use this comparison as a yardstick, to gauge the source and quality of our power.

If you get no inspiration or happiness from your efforts you certainly are not in the right attitude toward those about you. Correct this by discussion with other members, then center your attention and energy on some act *that will not benefit you but will help someone else*. This opens the channel of God's will and releases His power in you. You cannot fail in your purpose if you carry a God-consciousness with you.

Emotions must be taken into consideration in connection with our desire for power to carry out God's will.

The paradox of the alcoholic's emotions is complicated to the extent that they either make or break him.

There is a reasonable solution to this problem, however, one that responds to the intelligent application of facts that science has provided.

We know from experience that fear and anger had much to do in our acquiring and maintaining an alcoholic condition. It is generally understood that feelings of hate, criticism, resentment, self-pity, jealousy, intolerance and other such manifestations of emotions, or feelings prolonged and aggravated our alcoholic condition.

Psychology teaches us that EMOTIONS AND FEELINGS ARE SOURCES OF ENERGY. Examples of this energy are to be found in the emotions of SEX, FEAR, ANGER AND LOVE. We are further taught that man must have this emotional energy to function mentally and physically. Without it he would be abnormal.

We are also informed that without the drive of emotional energy man would be a helpless bed-ridden creature. He would lack the capacity to engage in the daily routine of living. He would not think or move about. He would be practically immobile. He would retain his reflex action, nothing else.

The simple deductions from these facts are that the alcoholic has overlooked the value of harnessing the right emotional energy. He has used the energy of negative power at the expense of positive energy.

Obviously, the drive from sex, fear and anger has been employed instinctively. Ironically we have concentrated on the power of these forces to the detriment of our own well-being. We have not taken the time to visualize our inability to withstand the demands of such concentrated energy.

We have overlooked the greater source of energy that we are capable of generating and can withstand, namely: LOVE.

The lasting inspiration of power and energy that we can withstand in happiness and comfort is found in the maternal instinct of all races. It is the force and drive of LOVE.

Human energy is at its maximum and is most constructive in form when the mind and body are activated by this worthy emotion.

It is reasonable to believe, therefore, that the POWER TO CARRY OUT GOD'S WILL MUST COME FROM THE INSPIRATION AND ENERGY THAT ARE TO BE FOUND IN THE EMOTION OF LOVE.

STEP TWELVE—*Having had a spiritual experience as the result of these steps, we tried to carry this message to alcoholics, and to practice these principles in all our affairs*

———

Step Twelve is exacting to a high degree, specifically pointing out that a spiritual awakening is possible *only* if we have been living each of the preceding steps, and then suggesting that we draw from our experience and knowledge an objective message which we convey to other interested alcoholics. It further advises us to continue the Alcoholics Anonymous program as a "Design for Living," as our future "Way of Life."

Interpretation and practical application of Step Twelve is simply arrived at by separate consideration of the three divisions into which this step falls.

## FIRST DIVISION

"*Having had a spiritual experience as the result of these steps.*"

The new member is slow to recognize a spiritual experience in his new "Way of Life;" in fact, the terms "Spiritual Experience" or "Awakening" often confuse him by diverting his thought from intended A.A. usage to halos, sprouting wings, religion, mystic phenomena, or drastic emotional upheavals.

Reference to pages 567 and 568, in Appendix 2 of the book, "Alcoholics Anonymous," clarify the meanings of these spiritual terms, explaining that revolutionary character changes are not common, but that as we do enlarge upon our spiritual concepts we can develop a God consciousness that will entirely change our reaction toward life and our attitude toward our fellow men.

In arriving at a true picture of this A.A. metamorphosis it is helpful to reflect upon our spiritual experience as steppingstones to the NEW PERSONALITIES we gain by daily practice of the Twelve Steps.

Most of our experiences are what the psychologist William James calls the "educational variety" because *they develop slowly over a period of time*. Quite often friends of the newcomer are aware of the difference long before he is himself. He finally realizes that he has undergone a profound alteration in his reaction to life; that such a change could hardly have been brought about by himself alone.

We then sense the handiwork of this POWER GREATER THAN OURSELVES as in a few months we have acquired sobriety, peace of mind and sane behavior that years of self-discipline could not bring.

It takes no great stretch of imagination to allocate the source of power we draw upon in arresting alcoholism; we should have little trouble recognizing, in the awareness of this power, the essence of spiritual experience.

Evidence of the help God has provided us can be detected in the humility we have acquired, the responsibility we daily assume; the contented sobriety we enjoy and the unselfish interest we take in aiding fellow alcoholics.

The restraint we exercise with regard to resentment, anger, criticism; the amends we make; our sincerity, honesty, tolerance, these are all possible because of our willingness to accept the spiritual concepts of our program.

Sobriety in itself is a miracle in our case. Looking back over our lives for the past few months we concede a decided improvement in our moral viewpoint. We have developed God-conscious personalities sufficient to effect our recovery from alcoholism. The changes that have made our recovery possible can be identified as spiritual experiences. They have altered seemingly impossible circumstances in our lives.

Anyone, who having been a member of Alcoholics Anonymous long enough to complete eleven steps, without a spiritual experience, is either dishonest with himself, or has completely missed the purpose of this program. He should discuss his case with some older, understanding member who can aid him in surmounting his difficulties.

### SECOND DIVISION

*"We tried to carry this message to alcoholics."*

Much well-meant but misguided effort by sincere members results when they fail to differentiate between "Carrying the Message" and "Working with Others."

"Working with others," commonly referred to as "Sponsorship," is the art of helping an alcoholic to arrest his illness.

Sponsorship amounts to a pact between two alcoholics in which one, admitting he is powerless over alcohol, requests help and supervision from the other, a seasoned, qualified A.A. member, who in turn, agrees that he will devote his best effort in helping the other to make A.A. philosophy his "way of life."

Sponsorship has to do with human life and happiness so is too serious a business to be trusted in the hands of any but a qualified member; success in handling the new man is always a problem, even under the best circumstances. We therefore feel that in justice to the new man it is imperative he be handled by an experienced sponsor. The qualification and technique of sponsorship are covered in a separate article.

The member who sponsors carries the message, but the member who carries the message does not necessarily sponsor.

By this we wish to imply that a member who has been in Alcoholics Anonymous thirty days can carry the message to other alcoholics, but he surely would not attempt to help straighten out another man's thinking, or sponsor him when he does not yet understand his own problem.

The question naturally arises, "What constitutes carrying the message to alcoholics; how far do we go in this respect?"

The list of suggested methods is not complete but will provide examples and at the same time serve as a basis of comparison for other ways that you may have in mind:

1.  The most convincing message you can present to intimate associates with alcoholic problems is your own normal, contented sobriety. This statement rules out the theory that the exhibitionist who seeks out his old drinking cronies to show them he can

indulge in soft drinks all night, is an approved method of carrying the message. We hold with the advice given by our founders in this respect. They say, "Assuming that we are spiritually fit, we can do all sorts of things alcoholics are not supposed to do." You will note that we have made an important qualification, therefore, ask yourself on each occasion, "Have I any good social, business, or personal reason for going to this place, or am I stealing a little vicarious pleasure from the atmosphere of such places?" But be sure that you are on solid spiritual ground before you start and that your motive in going is thoroughly good.

2. Admitting to someone that you are an alcoholic.

3. The story of your A.A. experience to professional men whom you know intimately, such as doctors, lawyers, judges, also men of the clergy.

4. Calls with older members who are sponsoring.

5.  The example of regular attendance at A.A. meetings. This includes out-of-town meetings when traveling.

6.  By becoming a part of the group and assuming responsibility.

7.  By assuming the responsibility of talking before A.A. groups if asked to help out with a program.

8.  By your obvious belief that you have received h e l p  f r o m  a POWER GREATER THAN YOURSELF.

9.  Hospital calls.

10. Telephone calls to new members.

11. Personal talks with members after meetings, particularly new members.

12. Talks with wives or relatives who are interested and ask for an understanding of how some member of their family might be benefited.

13. By the practice of tolerance and understanding of weaker members' problems which you attempt to help them overcome by constructive word or action.

14. By close observance and study of our

Twelve-Step Program as a means of qualifying for sponsorship.

15. By making a reasonable pledge of your time, money and energy.

16. By owning one or more books that you read yourself and lend to new members.

17. Distribution of our literature to interested people.

18. By advising all new members to own an A.A. book.

19. By making proper amends.

20. By admitting it when you are wrong.

## THIRD DIVISION

*"And to practice these principles in all our affairs."*

The principles of the Twelve Steps sum up to a logical, practical philosophy that when willingly and honestly lived, guarantees any alcoholic recovery from his disease.

Recovery is all that we can expect or ask for as we know that an alcoholic can never practice controlled drinking because his nervous system is not constituted to permit it.

The quest of the human race is sane behavior, useful endeavor, security, peace of mind and happiness; this is our rightful inheritance, but one which is denied the alcoholic so long as he fails to recognize in alcoholism a three-fold disease.

This inheritance is restored to him:

1. When he acknowledges his illness.

2. When he seeks help from a POWER GREATER THAN HIMSELF to arrest it.

3. When he studies and isolates his moral defects of character.

4. When he admits them to himself, God and another human being.

5. When he realizes the physical, mental and spiritual injury they have caused.

6. When he concedes the injury his self-centered drinking addiction has inflicted upon others.

7. When he asks God to forgive him for these injuries and is willing to make amends to those harmed.

8. When, having acquired happiness, sane behavior, useful living through so-

briety, he maintains it by a daily check-up on his progress and continues the conscious contact he has established with God.

9. When he shares the knowledge and experience of his recovery from alcoholism with other alcoholics who ask for help.

10. When he continues the practice of these principles in ALL HIS AFFAIRS.

31230857R00067

Made in the USA
Charleston, SC
11 July 2014